PLAY OF THE HAND
AS DECLARER
AND DEFENDER

Shirley Silverman

Revised by Pat Harrington
and Harry Silverman

Published by
BARON BARCLAY BRIDGE SUPPLIES
1-800-274-2221

INTRODUCTION

In bridge, as in life, you must "PLAN" to be successful. These lessons are designed to help you "PLAN" a hand when playing bridge — to "think through" the complexities of declarer play and defense. As your game improves and your skills increase, you will enjoy playing bridge even more than you do now. And you will win more, too. And be sure to remember the most important person at the table — your partner. Treat him with the courtesy and understanding that you expect in return — happy partnerships are winning partnerships. May yours always be both.

"HE & SHE"

The bridge student is consistently referred to as "he," not because of a bias against the "she's" in the class, but merely to make the text more readable.

ACKNOWLEDGMENTS

The author wishes to thank Marty Bergen of White Plains, N.Y., and Kit Woolsey of Arlington, Va., for many of the practice hands in this course. Bob Goldwater of Hartsdale, N.Y., and Peggy Mendes of Scarsdale, N.Y., were of great help in reading and editing the manuscript. Both Bob Mendelsohn's Adult Education classes in White Plains, N.Y., and my classes with the Continuing Education Program of Pleasantville, Briarcliff and Pocantico Hills, N.Y., were of invaluable help in testing the material.

S.S.S.

Baron Barclay Bridge Supplies
3600 Chamberlain Lane, Suite 206
Louisville, Kentucky 40241
1-800-274-2221
FAX 502-426-2044

CONTENTS

BRIDGE PROPRIETIES

An accepted code of bridge etiquette and bridge ethics has grown up during the centuries in which the game has been played. *There are no penalties for a breach of ethics.* Intentional violations of bridge proprieties are considered dishonest and ungentlemanly, but it is not within the scope of the bridge laws to penalize them.

DO NOT bid or play with special emphasis or use any inflection of the voice which would give partner information on the nature of your hand.

DO NOT watch the cards as they are being dealt. Do not draw inferences about the place in his hand from which another player pulls a card in playing.

DO NOT express displeasure (or satisfaction) at a lead, play, bid, double or any other call partner makes.

DO NOT draw any inferences from the fact that partner has hesitated, or has bid with any special emphasis or inflection.

DO NOT hesitate, either in the bidding or in the play, in order to deceive the opponents.

DO NOT use any conventional bids known to you and partner which have not been explained to the opponents. The term *conventional bid* refers to any bid (or double or redouble) which has a special meaning to your partner not generally used by the other players at the table.

DO NOT prepare to lead to a trick before the previous trick is completed, or to take in a trick before it is completed, since this may inform partner as to cards in your hand.

DO NOT announce the score in order to call partner's attention to the fact that you have a partscore and a lower bid than usual will be enough for game.

BUT: It is not your duty to call attention to your side's breach of law, such as a revoke made by you or your partner.

LESSON ONE

Play of the Hand in a Trump Contract

Handling the Trump Suit
Reducing Dummy's Ruffing Power
Making a Plan

MAKING A MASTER PLAN

1. How many losers are there in each suit?
2. How many losers can you afford?
3. How can some of these losers be eliminated?
4. Should trump be drawn immediately?

GAINING ADDITIONAL TRICKS IN THE TRUMP SUIT

You gain additional tricks by trumping in your shorter trump suit or crossruffing the entire hand.

MAKE THIS YOUR CREED FROM THIS MOMENT ON

*"I will always endeavor to play according to plan.
Any plan, no matter how poor, is superior to
no plan at all."*

AN AVERAGE PLAYER PARTNERSHIP WHOSE MUTUAL UNDERSTANDING IS STRONG CAN OFTTIMES WIN OVER TWO LIFE MASTERS WHO CAN'T "GET TOGETHER."

Hand A

Contract: 4♠
Lead: ♣K

Dummy
- ♠ QJ7
- ♥ AK532
- ♦ 6
- ♣ 9842

Declarer
- ♠ AK1098
- ♥ 94
- ♦ A832
- ♣ A3

(1) How many losers does declarer have in

Spades_____ Hearts_____

Diamonds_____ Clubs_____

(2) How can declarer eliminate some of the losers?

_____

_____

(3) Should declarer draw trump immediately? _____

(4) Will declarer gain tricks by trumping in his own hand? ____

(5) Why? _____

_____

_____

_____

(1) Spades, 0; hearts, 0; diamonds, 3; clubs, 1. (2) Use the trump in the North hand to ruff diamonds. (3) No. (4) No. (5) Trumping in the long trump suit does not gain tricks.

YOU DO NOT GAIN ADDITIONAL TRICKS BY TRUMPING WITH YOUR LONGER TRUMP SUIT. EACH OF THESE CARDS IS ALREADY A TRICK.

North

9	8	7	6	
A	7	4	2	

South

1	2	3	4	5
K	Q	J	10	3

The five spades in South's hand will always take five tricks. However, each trump in the North hand that South can use "independently" will score an additional trick.

REVOKES

Revoke: To fail to follow suit when a card of the suit led is in your hand.

Established Revoke: When you or your partner have led or played to the next trick after committing a revoke.

Penalties (2003 Laws of Contract Bridge)

Case 1: Offending side did not win revoke trick or any subsequent tricks — no penalty. **Case 2**: Offending side won only one trick after the revoke occurred (including the revoke trick) — one trick penalty. **Case 3**: Offending side won two or more tricks after the revoke occurred (including the revoke trick) — immediately transfer one trick; a second trick is transferred if the revoker (not his partner or the non-offenders) won the revoke trick or the revoker wins a later trick with a card of the revoke suit.

No additional penalty is paid for a further revoke in the same suit by the same player. N.B. If a revoke causes damage to the offending side insufficiently compensated by this law, additional tricks should be transferred to restore equity.

No revoke can be established on trick twelve and thirteen. The player must withdraw the offending card and play the card he is legally obliged to play.

There is no revoke penalty if the revoke is discovered after the cards have been mixed together at the end of the hand.

Hand B

Contract: 4♠
Lead: ♣K

Dummy
- ♠ QJ82
- ♥ AK32
- ♦ 6
- ♣ 9842

Declarer
- ♠ AK109
- ♥ 94
- ♦ A8532
- ♣ A3

(6) How many losers does declarer have in

Spades _____ Hearts _____

Diamonds _____ Clubs _____

(7) How can declarer eliminate some of the losers?

_____

_____

(8) Should declarer draw trump? _____

(9) How does Hand A differ from Hand B? _____

_____

(10) What precaution should declarer take early? _____

_____

(11) Why? _____

_____

_____

(6) Spades, 0; hearts, 0; diamonds, 4; clubs, 1. (7) Trump them. (8) No. (9) South will need to use trump as entries (a cross ruff). (10) Play the heart ace and king. (11) To keep the opponents from trumping them, which they may do if they can discard hearts on repeated diamond leads.

WHEN THE BIDDING INDICATES THAT DUMMY WILL HAVE A SHORT SUIT, AN OPENING TRUMP LEAD IS OFTEN EFFECTIVE.

WHEN YOU HAVE NO STRENGTH IN DECLARER'S SEC-OND SUIT, ALWAYS CONSIDER THE POSSIBILITY THAT PARTNER MAY HAVE STRENGTH IN THE SUIT, AND PLAN YOUR DEFENSE ACCORDINGLY.

WHEN YOU SEE A SHORT SUIT IN DUMMY, CONSIDER SWITCHING TO A TRUMP.

Hand C

The bidding has gone:

Declarer	You	Dummy	Partner
1♥	Pass	1NT	Pass
2♣	Pass	Pass	Pass

(12) Does declarer have more hearts or more clubs? _____

(13) Does dummy have more hearts or more clubs? _____

(14) How do you know this? _____

_____

(15) Could a trump lead be effective? _____

(16) Why? _____

(12) Declarer's length in hearts and clubs could be equal but he will often have more hearts. (13) More clubs. (14) He chose clubs over hearts by passing. (15) Yes. (16) Declarer plans to trump his losing hearts with dummy's clubs.

9

Hand D

The bidding has gone:

Declarer	You	Dummy	Partner
1♥	Pass	1NT	Pass
2♣	Pass	2♥	Pass
Pass	Pass		

(17) Does declarer have more hearts or more clubs? _____

_____

(18) Does dummy have more hearts or more clubs? _____

_____

(19) Could dummy have equal length in hearts and clubs?

_____

(20) Why did he choose hearts as the final contract?_____

_____

(21) Does dummy have three hearts? _____

(22) Could a trump lead be effective? _____

(23) Why? _____

_____

(17) Declarer is likely to have more hearts. (18) Cannot tell for sure from the bidding. (19) Yes. (20) With equal length in both suits, dummy returns opener to original suit. (21) Unlikely; with a weak hand dummy would probably have bid two hearts immediately. (22) Yes. (23) To prevent declarer from trumping losing clubs.

CONTRACT BRIDGE SCORING

EACH TRICK OVER SIX:

	Club	Diamond	Heart	Spade
	20	20	30	30

SUITS

If doubled, multiply by two; if redoubled, multiply by four.

NOTRUMP

1st Trick	Each subsequent trick
40	30

OVERTRICKS:	Not Vulnerable	Vulnerable
Undoubled, each...............	Trick Value	Trick Value
Doubled, each	100	200
Redoubled, each	200	400

SLAMS:		
Small slam	500	750
Grand slam	1000	1500

HONORS		
(If held in one hand)	Four honors 100
	Five honors 150
	Four aces at notrump 150

UNDERTRICKS:

	Not Vulnerable		Vulnerable	
	Undoubled	Doubled	Undoubled	Doubled
1st undertrick	50	100	100	200
Second and third undertricks	50	200	100	300
Each subsequent undertrick	50	300	100	300

If redoubled, multiply doubled value by two.

Premiums

Winning first two games: 700. Winning two out of three: 500.
Unfinished rubber (one game): 300.
Winner of score in unfinished game: 100.
Making a doubled contract: 50.
Making a redoubled contract: 100.

(24) How many points does your side earn if it bids two spades and makes four?_____

(25) How many of these points go below the line? _____

(26) How many of these points go above the line? _____

(27) What is your side's rubber bonus if each side has scored a game and you score the third game? _____

(28) How many points do you get if you bid two clubs not vulnerable, are doubled, and make an overtrick? _____

(29) Which of these points goes below the line? _____

(30) What bonus do you get for making a doubled contract?

_____

(31) What bonus do you get for making an overtrick, doubled, vulnerable? _____

(32) If your opponents are vulnerable and you double them and set them four tricks, how many points do you get? _____

(24) 120 points. (25) 60 points. (26) 60 points. (27) 500 points.
(28) 230 points. (29) 80 points. (30) 50 points. (31) 200 points.
(32) 1100 points.

LESSON TWO

Planning the Play of a Hand
Finessing to Produce Winners

THE FINESSE

If you lead a low card toward an ace-queen combination and play the ace, you have virtually no chance to avoid losing to the king later. Playing the queen in this situation is called "taking a finesse" — you now have a fifty-fifty chance of winning two tricks. There are many types of finesses; following are some finesse combinations. If you hold the cards on the lower line in each case and dummy has the cards on the upper line, what card should you lead in each example? What card should you play from dummy if your left hand opponent follows with a low card? A WINNING HINT: When leading for a finesse, lead a high card only when you would like your opponent to cover if he can.

(1) A 7 4   Lead? _____   (5) A K 5   Lead? _____
     Q J 10 Dummy? ___   J 10 9 Dummy? ___

(2) K 9 3   Lead? _____   (6) K J 4   Lead? _____
     J 10 8 Dummy? ___   8 6 2   Dummy? ___

(3) A Q 10 Lead? _____   (7) A J 10 Lead? _____
     J 9 8   Dummy? ___   7 6 2   Dummy? ___

(4) K 5   Lead? _____   (8) K J 9   Lead? _____
     3 2   Dummy? ___   10 6 2 Dummy? ___

(1) Queen, four. (2) Jack, three. (3) Jack, ten. (4) Two, king.
(5) Jack, five. (6) Two, jack. (7) Two, ten. (8) Ten, nine.

(9) What is the correct first play with this combination?

A 8 3

_____

Q 7 4

(10) What should be played next? _____

(11) Why? _____

(9) Play the ace. (10) Lead toward the queen. (11) Hope your right hand opponent has the king.

DETERMINING SURE AND POSSIBLE LOSERS IN A SUIT CONTRACT

SURE LOSERS MUST ALWAYS BE LOST. For example:

A missing ace, if you cannot trump it.

Two trump tricks (at least) if you are missing the ace, queen and jack.

POSSIBLE LOSERS INCLUDE **ALL** CARDS THAT ARE NOT SURE WINNERS. Possible losers are losers that may be avoided by careful declarer play — through a finesse, by trumping in dummy, a discard, or through a favorable split of the opponents' cards.

The queen in an ace-queen combination is one possible loser.

A king-jack combination opposite a worthless doubleton is one sure and one possible loser.

HOW TO BECOME A POPULAR BRIDGE PARTNER

Be a congenial partner.

Do not give lessons to your partner and opponents.

Adjust your bridge to the calibre of your partner's game. If your partner lacks experience, do not make bids which will be over his head.

Do not "hog" the bidding. (The "hog" usually is the persistent notrump bidder.)

Do not be a sore loser.

14

Contract: 4♠
Lead: ♥Q

Dummy
- ♠ AQ75
- ♥ 862
- ♦ K98
- ♣ K82

Declarer
- ♠ J10932
- ♥ AK3
- ♦ 75
- ♣ AQ5

(12) How many sure losers in:

Spades _____   Hearts _____

Diamonds _____   Clubs _____

(13) How many other possible losers in:

Spades _____   Hearts _____

Diamonds _____   Clubs _____

(14) Should trump be drawn immediately? ____

(15) Which finesses will you take _____

(16) Can you make your contract if all of your finesses lose? ___

(17) Why? _____

(12) Spades, 0; hearts, 0; diamonds, 1; clubs, 1; (13) Spades, 1; hearts, 0; diamonds, 1; clubs, 0. (14) Yes. (15) Spades and diamonds. (16) No. (17) You will lose four tricks, one in spades, two in diamonds and one in hearts.

Contract: 4♠
Lead: ♥K

Dummy
- ♠ Q743
- ♥ 6
- ♦ KJ32
- ♣ 9643

Declarer
- ♠ KJ10952
- ♥ A42
- ♦ A10
- ♣ 52

(18) How many sure losers in:

Spades _____   Hearts _____

Diamonds _____   Clubs _____

(19) How many other possible losers in:

Spades _____   Hearts _____

Diamonds _____   Clubs _____

(20) Should trump be drawn at once? _____

(21) Why? _____

(22) Is there a right way to finesse the diamond? _____

(18) Spades, 1; hearts, 0; diamonds, 0; clubs, 2. (19) Spades, 0; hearts, 2; diamonds, 0; clubs, 0. (20) No. (21) Two losing hearts must be trumped in dummy. (22) A diamond finesse should not be taken. If you take the finesse and it loses, you will lose four tricks — one spade, two clubs and a diamond. If the finesse wins you would only make an overtrick. NEVER JEOPARDIZE A CONTRACT FOR AN OVERTRICK.

Contract: 4♥
Lead: ♦K

Dummy
- ♠ AQ965
- ♥ 762
- ♦ 6
- ♣ 8752

Declarer
- ♠ 32
- ♥ KQJ1098
- ♦ A73
- ♣ AQ

(23) How many sure losers in:

Spades _____   Hearts _____

Diamonds _____   Clubs _____

(24) How many other possible losers in:

Spades _____   Hearts _____

Diamonds _____   Clubs _____

(25) Should trump be attacked first? _____

(26) Why? _____

(27) Should the spade finesse be taken immediately? _____

(28) Why? _____

_____

(29) After declarer trumps a diamond, how should he return to

his hand? _____

(30) Should the club finesse be taken at this time? _____

(31) Why? _____

(32) What three losers is declarer willing to concede? _____

_____

(23) Spades, 0; hearts, 1; diamonds, 0; clubs, 0. (24) Spades, 1; hearts, 0; diamonds, 2; clubs, 1. (25) No. (26) Diamonds must be trumped in dummy. (27) No. (28) If it loses and the ace and another trump are played declarer will have a "sure" diamond loser; if the club finesse then fails he will not make his contract. (29) By playing to the ace of clubs. (30) No. (31) Same reason that the spade finesse was not taken. (32) King of spades, king of clubs and ace of hearts.

16

DETERMINING WINNERS IN A NOTRUMP CONTRACT

Declarer counts losers in a suit contract because he is able to trump once he runs out of cards in a suit. In notrump contracts, declarer continues to lose tricks even after he runs out of cards in a suit. It is easier to plan the play in notrump by counting winners.

In a notrump contract, declarer should first determine how many winners he can take IMMEDIATELY. If this number corresponds to his contract then he should take his tricks. If declarer needs more tricks than he can immediately take he must work out a plan to take the additional trick or tricks — setting up a long suit, taking one or more finesses, etc. Declarer should do the work necessary to set up needed tricks immediately.

Examine this hand and determine how many immediate winners declarer has in each suit:

Contract: 3NT
Lead: ♠Q

Dummy
♠ K76
♥ AQ32
♦ 85
♣ K432

Declarer
♠ A982
♥ K54
♦ AK
♣ QJ109

(33) Spades? _____

(34) Hearts? _____

(35) Diamonds? _____

(36) Clubs? _____

(37) From what suit will declarer's additional

tricks come? _____

(38) When should declarer attack clubs? _____

(37) Clubs. (38) As soon as he gains the lead.
(33) Spades, 2. (34) Hearts, 3. (35) Diamonds, 2. (36) Clubs, 0.

LESSON THREE

Setting up a Long Suit
Preserving Entries
Holdup Plays by Defenders
Giving Count

"GIVING THE COUNT" TELLS PARTNER
HOW MANY CARDS YOU HOLD IN A SUIT

GIVING COUNT IS COMPLETELY ETHICAL.

GIVING COUNT IS A NECESSARY TOOL FOR WIN-
NING DEFENSE.

(Never "slam" your card onto the table. Giving count is done
"visually," not "audibly.")

TO SIGNAL AN <u>EVEN</u> NUMBER OF CARDS, PLAY A
HIGH CARD AND THEN A LOW CARD.

TO SIGNAL AN <u>ODD</u> NUMBER OF CARDS, PLAY YOUR
CARDS "UP THE LINE."

1	2		4	1	3	2		
9	**7**		**9**	**7**	**4**	**3**		
3	2	1	5	4	3	2	1	
8	**7**	**2**	**8**	**7**	**5**	**3**	**2**	

GIVE COUNT WHEN IT IS IMPORTANT FOR PARTNER
TO KNOW HOW MANY CARDS YOU HAVE IN A SUIT.
THIS IS ESPECIALLY TRUE WHEN DECLARER IS TRY-
ING TO SET UP A SUIT (USUALLY IN THE DUMMY) AND
THERE IS NO OUTSIDE ENTRY TO IT.

In what order do you play the following cards to give partner count?

(1) 8 7 6 4 _____   (2) 8 7 6 4 3 2 _____

(3) 7 4 _____   (4) 9 8 4 3 2 _____   (5) 8 7 5 _____

(1) Play the 8 followed by the 4. (2) Play the 8 followed by the 2. (3) 7 4. (4) 2 3 4 8 9. (5) 5 7 8.

HOLDUP PLAY

A holdup play is made when you delay taking a trick, usually because you wish to cut communications between your opponents' hands. For example, with a long suit in the dummy and no outside entry you would delay taking your ace (if you could) until declarer played his last card in the suit. You hope that declarer cannot make his contract without the tricks that are stranded in dummy.

The contract is three notrump and this is your hand:

♠ 92
♥ 5432
♦ A62
♣ KQJ10

(6) What is your opening lead? _____

(7) Declarer has a long diamond suit in the dummy headed by the K Q J 10 8 and no outside entry. When declarer leads a low diamond toward the dummy, do you take your ace? _____

(8) Why? _____

_____

(9) How can partner help? _____

_____

(6) King of clubs. (7) No. (8) You must hold up until declarer has played the last diamond from his hand. (9) By giving count in the diamond suit.

The contract is three notrump and this is your hand:

♠ 92
♥ 543
♦ A62
♣ KQJ109

(10) What is your opening lead? _____

(11) The same conditions prevail as in the previous hand, and declarer once again leads a low diamond. Do you take your ace? _____

(12) Why? _____

_____

(10) King of clubs. (11) Yes. (12) You need five tricks to set the contract and you should take them immediately. (Partner will not thank you if your holdup play allows them to make their contract.)

The contract is three notrump and this is your hand:

♠ J2
♥ 5432
♦ A62
♣ KQJ10

(13) What is your opening lead? _____

(14) Declarer has a long diamond suit in the dummy headed by the K Q J 10 8 plus the queen of spades. Declarer leads a low diamond toward the dummy. Do you take your ace?

_____

(15) Why? _____

_____

(13) King of clubs. (14) No. (15) You must hold up until declarer has played the last diamond from his hand. You must hope that partner has the king of spades (or the ace) so that declarer will be denied an entry to the established suit.

AS DECLARER IN A TRUMP CONTRACT

BEFORE you play to the first trick, decide on a line of play. Count your "SURE" and "POSSIBLE" losers, look at your entries and your long suits, decide if trump should be drawn immediately or whether you must use trump to avoid losers. Must finesses be taken? If so, WHEN is important. Are there entries to take finesses?

PLAN BEFORE YOU PLAY . . . THE WRONG CARD AT TRICK ONE CAN COST YOU THE CONTRACT. YOU WILL CERTAINLY HAVE TO STOP AND THINK AT SOME TIME; SUCCESSFUL PLAYERS THINK THROUGH

A HAND **BEFORE** THEY PLAY TO TRICK ONE AS DE-
CLARER. LONGER AND LONGER HESITATIONS AS
THE PLAY OF THE HAND PROGRESSES ARE USUALLY
NONPRODUCTIVE (and annoying to your opponents, too).
Every plan you make will not work — unfriendly distribution as
well as clever defenders will see to that. However, start planning
early. As you gain experience, more and more of your plans will
work.

Contract: 4♥   (16) How many sure losers does declarer have?
Lead: ♦Q
_____

Dummy   (17) In what suits are these? _____
♠ J82
♥ 764   (18) How many possible losers are there? _____
♦ A6
♣ KQJ102   (19) In what suits are these? _____

Declarer   (20) Where should declarer win the first
♠ Q54
♥ AKJ92   trick?____
♦ K32
♣ 84   (21) Why? _____

(22) Name three possible lines of play _____

_____

(23) Which is best and why? _____

(24) Must the heart finesse be taken? _____

(25) If yes, why? _____

(16) 3. (17) 3. Spades, 2; clubs, 1. (18) 3. (19) Spades, 1; hearts, 1;
diamonds, 1. (20) In his hand. (21) To preserve dummy's entry. (22)
Set up the club suit, go to dummy and finesse for the heart queen,
trump the losing diamond in dummy. (23) Lead a club. If your
opponents take the ace, you take the heart finesse as soon as you
regain the lead. The balance of the clubs will give you enough
tricks to make the contract (if the heart finesse works). If they don't
take the ace of clubs, take the heart finesse immediately; if it wins
then go back to the club suit. (25) Because it must succeed
for the contract to make as the defense can always win two spades
and the club ace. (However, without club discards you will probably
lose three spades and the club ace.)

21

LESSON FOUR

Cooperative Defense:
The Arts of Leading
and Signalling

WHEN DEFENDING, AN ALERT PARTNERSHIP:
  I. **Listens to and remembers the bidding**
     1. **Is declarer's or dummy's point count limited?**
     2. **Do you know anything about your opponents' distribution?**
     3. **What do you know about partner's hand?**
     4. **What conclusions can you make after dummy is tabled?**
  II. **Watches declarer's line of play**
     1. **Can you pinpoint declarer's main weakness or weaknesses?**
     2. **Can you determine declarer's line of play?**
  III. **Cooperates with partner's line of play**
     1. **Signals when appropriate**
     2. **Carefully watches each card partner plays**
     3. **Endeavors to come up with a line of defense which will defeat the contract**

PARTNER'S BIDDING (OR FAILURE TO BID) CAN TELL YOU A LOT ABOUT HIS HAND, IF YOU TAKE THE TIME TO THINK ABOUT IT.

In each of these sequences, what is partner's maximum point count and how do you know this?

	You	Opponent	Partner	Opponent
(1)	1♦	1NT	Pass	2NT
	Pass	3NT	Pass	Pass
	Pass			
(2)	1NT	Pass	Pass	2♥
	Pass	Pass	Pass	
(3)	1♥	1♠	Pass	3♠
	Pass	4♠	Pass	Pass
	Pass			
(4)	1♠	1NT	Pass	2♥
	Pass	Pass	Pass	
(5)	1♣	Pass	Pass	1♠
	Pass	3♠	Pass	Pass
	Pass			

(1) About one point; you have an opening bid and your opponents have twenty-six points. Partner probably has a jack. (2) Seven. With eight points partner would have responded to your opening bid. (3) Very little, since your opponents have reached game despite your opening bid. (4) Five or perhaps a bit more since your opponents have not bid a game. (Partner may not have been able to make a bid over the one notrump overcall.) (5) Five; with six points partner would not have passed your opening bid.

OPENING LEADS IN SUIT CONTRACTS

1. Top of an honor sequence Q J 10 9,   K Q J,   A K 3*
2. Low from an honor Q 4 3. (But don't lead low from an ace.)
3. Top of a doubleton 9 6,   K 5
4. Top of nothing 9 7 6**

*Some players lead the king from this holding.
**Some players prefer to lead low or middle from three small.

OPENING LEADS IN NOTRUMP CONTRACTS

LEAD PARTNER'S SUIT IF PARTNER HAS BID
1. Top of a sequence headed by two or more honors
     Q J 4,   K Q 7
2. Top of a doubleton 9 6, K 5
3. Low from three or more headed by an honor
     Q 6 4,   A 7 5 3
4. Top of nothing 7 4 3

LEAD YOUR OWN LONG SUIT WHEN PARTNER HAS NOT BID
1. Top of sequence of three or more honors
     Q J 10 7 5,   K Q J 5
2. Top of a broken sequence Q J 9 8 2
3. Top of an interior sequence
     A J 10 9 8,   K J 10 9 8,   A Q J 10 3
4. With no sequence, lead fourth best.
     A J 9 6 3,   K 10 6 5

PARTNER OF OPENING LEADER

1. Play third hand high to try to win the trick when the lead is a low card.
2. Show attitude when the lead is an honor or when dummy wins the trick. Play a HIGH CARD to tell partner to continue the suit; play a LOW CARD to show no interest in the suit. (Partner can still continue if he thinks that is best.)

Assume that you have agreed to lead the top of touching honors. Unless it is obvious that partner will have to make a shift after winning the first trick with his honor, it is your duty to show whether or not you like his suit. If you have an honor that continues partner's sequence, you should encourage partner to lead the suit again. If you have a doubleton and can trump before declarer draws your trumps, encourage partner to continue the suit. (Sometimes this will require you to overtake partner's king with your ace.)

The contract is four spades. Partner leads the queen of hearts; dummy has the 9 3 2. What do you play with each of these holdings?

(6) A 8 4 _____   (7) K 8 4 _____   (8) 8 4 _____

(9) K 8 _____   (10) A 8 _____   (11) A K 8 _____

(6) Ace; don't risk letting declarer win a singleton king. (7) Eight. (8) Four; even though you have a doubleton, you probably won't get to ruff a heart before trumps are drawn. (9) King. (10) Ace. (11) King; then play the ace. If it holds, return the eight. If this had been a notrump contract, this play would be crucial to prevent blocking the suit.

The contract is four spades. Suppose partner leads the king of diamonds, promising the queen; dummy has the 9 3 2. What do you play with each of these holdings?

(12) A 8 4_____   (13) J 8 4 _____   (14) 8 4 _____

(15) A 8 _____   (16) 8 4 3 _____   (17) A 8 7 4_____

(12) Eight. (13) Eight; the jack continues partner's sequence (however pairs who lead the king from both king-queen and ace-king should not encourage with the jack since it is not clear who has the queen.) (14) Four; partner doesn't have the ace so you can't trump immediately. (Pairs who lead the king from both ace-king and king-queen should encourage in the hope that partner has the ace.) (15) Ace. (16) Three. (17) Eight.

DURING THE PLAY OF THE HAND

1. If partner needs to know how many cards you have in a suit,
   GIVE COUNT:

   > HIGH-LOW = Even Number of Cards
   > LOW-HIGH = Odd Number of Cards

2. If you cannot follow to a trick and want partner to shift to a particular suit, DISCARD A HIGH CARD IN THAT SUIT. Likewise, the discard of a low card says you do not want that suit led.

3. If declarer is drawing trump and you wish to show partner that you have three trump and that you desire to trump something, play your trump in this fashion:

	1	2		1		2
9	4	2*		8	7	3

   *The 9 may be too valuable to use as a signal.

DO NOT PLAY TO THE FIRST TRICK (REGARDLESS OF HOW OBVIOUS THE PLAY IS) WITHOUT THINKING. THIS IS A VITAL HABIT WHICH MUST BECOME AUTOMATIC.

Whether you are a declarer or defender you should try to place the high cards; the bidding will aid in revealing this information. Your plan of play will not always follow a straight course. Do not become flustered if you discover unfavorable distribution; stop and modify your play to meet new and unexpected developments. With experience, you will be able to make changes in your plan of play.

Do not become discouraged if your plans go awry at first — very often intermediate players will pursue the first plan that comes to mind, without realizing a safer and surer procedure of play is also there to be developed. Learn to ask yourself, "Is this the only and best plan?" As time progresses, you will find the results of your "studying out the cards" very gratifying.

LESSON FIVE

Blocking and Unblocking

WHEN TO PLAY YOUR HONOR CARD ON PARTNER'S HONOR

1. To show partner the location of a missing honor.
2. To retain an entry into partner's hand so that partner can later "run" his suit.
3. To force declarer to use his stopper, permitting partner to overtake your low card on a later round and continue the suit.

Your first thought when partner leads an honor should be "What cards does partner hold?" Look at the dummy and your own cards and you will know, in most cases, who holds the missing honors. Use this knowledge to "HELP" partner.

DEFENSIVE UNBLOCKING ON OPENING LEADS AGAINST NOTRUMP CONTRACTS

Compulsory Plays — (Lead of an unbid suit)

ACE asks you to drop an honor; with no honor give count.

KING asks for attitude.
  Exception: If holding the ace doubleton overtake the king and return the suit

QUEEN asks for the jack. (Partner has K Q 10 9.)

Partner leads a queen against a notrump contract. Dummy has three small cards.

(1) What other cards does partner likely hold? _____

(2) Could partner have the king? _____

(3) Could partner have the ace? _____

(4) You hold the K 9 5, which card do you play? _____

(5) You hold the K 9, which card do you play? _____

(6) You hold the A 8 5, which card do you play? _____

(7) You hold the A 8, which card do you play? _____

(1) Jack, ten. (2) Yes (but only with K Q 10 9). (3) Yes (The queen is the correct lead from A Q J 10). (4) Nine. (5) King. (6) Ace. (7) Ace. The ace MUST be played in (7) to unblock the suit. It is also the preferred answer in (6) as it removes all ambiguity as to the location of the ace, knowledge that should prove of great value to your partner.

**IF YOU BID A SUIT AND PARTNER LEADS
AN HONOR, IT MAY BE FROM A DOUBLETON
OR THE TOP OF A SEQUENCE ... for example,**

Q 3   Q J   Q J 8

DEFENSIVE UNBLOCKING ON OPENING LEAD AGAINST A SUIT CONTRACT

Decide what card(s) partner holds and play accordingly. Signal attitude but unblock with shortness after an honor lead.

UNBLOCKING DURING THE PLAY OF THE CONTRACT

Declarer **MUST UNBLOCK WHERE NECESSARY** in order to preserve entries.

Defenders **MUST UNBLOCK TO PRESERVE ENTRIES**, while never forgetting how many tricks their side needs to defeat the contract.

UNBLOCKING PLAYS IN SUIT CONTRACTS

PARTNER LEADS	DUMMY SHOWS	YOU HOLD
Q (J 10 x)	x x x	K 9
Q (J 10 x) x)	A x x Declarer plays low	K 9
Q (J 10 x)	A x x Declarer plays ace	K 9
Q (J 10 x)	x x x	A x
Q (J 10 x)	x x x	A 8 x
(K) J (10 9 x)	x x	A 8 2
(K) J (10 9 x)	Q x x	A 8 2

EVEN WHEN THE CONTRACT SEEMS IMPREGNABLE, REMEMBER THAT YOUR OPPONENTS ARE NOT INFALLIBLE. THEY TOO CAN MAKE MISTAKES. MANY GOOD CONTRACTS HAVE BEEN SET BY A POOR PLAY BY THE DECLARER. GIVE HIM AN OPPORTUNITY AND KEEP YOUR FINGERS CROSSED. LIKEWISE, POOR DEFENSE CAN ALLOW DECLARER TO MAKE A CONTRACT THAT SHOULD BE SET. NEVER SAY DIE!

When partner leads the queen against a suit contract and you have the king, it is vital to let him know this. With a doubleton YOU MUST IMMEDIATELY UNBLOCK THE KING. When partner leads a queen and you have the ace (and the king is not in dummy) it is once again important to play the ace. If declarer has a doubleton king, he is assured of a trick anyway; if he has a singleton king then you will get no tricks in the suit if you do not take your ace at one.

Partner leads a king against a notrump contract:

(8) What other cards does partner probably hold? _____

(9) You hold the A 9 5, which card do you play? _____

(10) You hold the A 9, which card do you play? _____

(8) Queen, jack. (9) Ace or signal with the 9. (10) Ace, for the same reasons that were valid in (7) in the previous question.

Partner leads an ace against a notrump contract:

(11) You hold the Q 9 4, which card do you play? _____

(12) Why? _____

(11) Queen. (12) Partner should hold A K J 10 and is asking you to unblock.

Your opponents are playing four spades. Partner leads the queen of diamonds and dummy has the 7 5 4. What do you play with?

(13) K 6 _____   (14) K 6 2 _____   (15) A 6 _____   (16) A 6 2 _____

(13) King. (14) Six. (15) Ace. (16) Ace.

Partner leads the king of diamonds and dummy has the 7 5 4. What do you play with?

(17) A 6 _____   (18) A 6 2 _____   (19) J 6 2 _____   (20) 9 6 2 _____

(17) Ace. (18) Ace. (19) Six (as long as the lead of the king shows the queen). (20) Two.

Against a contract of three notrump, partner leads the under-lined card and a small card is played from dummy. What do you play in each case?

PARTNER	YOU	
(21) Q (J 10 8 2)	K 7	____
(22) Q (J 10 8 2)	K 7 4	____
(23) Q (J 10 8 2)	A 4	____
(24) Q (J 10 8 2)	A 7 4	____
(25) K (Q J 8 2)	A 7	____
(26) A (K J 10 8)	Q 7 5	____
(27) K (Q J 8 2)	10 9 3	____
(28) K (Q J 8 2)	A 10 3	____
(29) K (Q J 8 2)	A 7	____
(30) Q (K 10 9)	J 6 2	____

(21) King. (22) King, though the seven would not be wrong. (23) Ace. (24) Ace, though the seven would not be wrong. (25) Ace. (26) Queen. (27) Ten. (28) Ten or ace. (29) Ace. (30) Jack.

IN A NOTRUMP CONTRACT COUNT YOUR SURE WINNERS.

IN A SUIT CONTRACT COUNT YOUR SURE AND POSSIBLE LOSERS.

AS DECLARER IN A TRUMP CONTRACT

DRAW TRUMP IF DUMMY'S TRUMPS ARE NOT NEEDED TO RUFF LOSERS.

SET UP A SIDE SUIT, IF ENTRIES ARE AVAILABLE.

TAKE FINESSES.

WATCH ENTRIES.

UNBLOCK TO CREATE ENTRIES; HOLD UP WINNERS TO CUT OPPONENTS' COMMUNICATION.

USE INFORMATION AVAILABLE FROM OPPONENTS' BID-DING AND PLAY.

AS DEFENDER AGAINST A TRUMP CONTRACT:

USE INFORMATION AVAILABLE FROM OPPONENTS' BID-DING TO MAKE A CONSTRUCTIVE OPENING LEAD.

USE SIGNALS TO HELP PLAN AN EFFECTIVE DEFENSE.

UNBLOCK AND HOLDUP WHEN NEEDED.

USE REPEATED TRUMP LEADS WHEN DECLARER SEEMS LIKELY TO MAKE ADDITIONAL TRICKS BY TRUMPING OR DECLARER ATTEMPTS TO CROSSRUFF OUT AN ENTIRE HAND.

LESSON SIX

Listening and Watching

PREEMPTIVE BIDS are opening bids on the two- or three-level (or higher). When your side preempts it can be all fun and games as you watch your opponents struggle to reach their optimum contract. Often your bid keeps them from an easily makable game, or they bid so high that they are in an unmakable contract.

Of course, when your opponents preempt, the shoe is on a different foot, and you have to struggle to get a good result. Realize that preemptive bids often do serve their purpose, and that when they are made against you, your results will not always be satisfying. Since world championship players often have trouble with such bids, there is no reason for you to feel disheartened when you get a bad score. Just remember the times when you make life difficult for your opponents with your high level bids.

REVIEW OF PREEMPTIVE THREE-LEVEL OPENING BIDS

Promises seven cards in the bid suit.
Does not have the values for an opening bid.
Will probably go down three tricks if not vulnerable and   two tricks if vulnerable, provided partner has no quick   tricks.
Partner bids a major suit game with three tricks if vulnerable,
    four tricks if not vulnerable — or with a weak hand in the
    hope of keeping opponents out of their optimum contract.
Partner bids a minor suit game with four tricks if vulnerable,
    five tricks if not vulnerable — or with a weak hand in the
    hope of keeping opponents out of their optimum contract.

DO NOT OPEN A HAND PREEMPTIVELY WHEN YOU HAVE THE VALUES FOR AN OPENING BID OF ONE IN A SUIT.

North	East	South	West
3♥	3♠	Pass	4♠
Pass	Pass	Pass	

(1) How many hearts does North have? _____

(2) If East wants to locate missing honors OUTSIDE the heart suit, in which hand are these likely to be found? _____

(3) Why? _____

_____

(1) Seven. (2) South. (3) If North had a long heart suit plus outside strength he would have opened one heart.

34

North	East	South	West
3♠	Pass	4♠	Pass
Pass	Pass		

(4) Does East know if South has a strong hand? _____

(5) Why? _____

_____

(6) What fact must East keep in mind when defending against

four spades? _____

_____

(7) Are holdup plays usually effective against preempting opponents? _____

(8) Why? _____

_____

(4) No. (5) The bid could be either based on strength or be made as a further preemptive bid. (6) Declarer probably has a seven card suit. (7) No. (8) Declarer is probably very short in one or more suits. You must take your aces and kings as soon as you can.

WHEN YOUR OPPONENTS OPEN THE BIDDING AND YOU BECOME DECLARER . . .

WHEN YOUR SIDE OPENS THE BIDDING AND YOUR OPPONENT BECOMES DECLARER . . .

USE THE BIDDING TO HELP YOU PLACE OUTSTANDING CARDS,

USE THE BIDDING TO HELP YOU MAKE DEDUCTIONS ABOUT DISTRIBUTION.

The bidding has gone:

Opponent	Partner	Opponent	You
1♠	Double	Pass	3♥
Pass	4♥	Pass	Pass
Pass			

Here is your hand and the dummy:

Dummy
♠ 85
♥ AQJ6
♦ KJ97
♣ A75

You
♠ QJ2
♥ 109742
♦ A104
♣ K2

(9) Which are your sure losers? _____

_____

(10) What should you play when your left hand opponent cashes the ace and king of spades and leads a third spade?

_____

(11) Why? _____

_____

(12) In what suits do you have possible losers? _____

(13) How can you attempt to avoid them? _____

(14) Which suit should be played first? _____

(15) Why? _____

(16) What would it mean if your right hand opponent turned out to have the king of hearts?

_____

_____

(17) If your left hand opponent turns out to have the king of hearts, what does this mean?

_____

_____

(9) Two spade tricks. (10) Either the queen or jack of hearts. (11) If your right hand opponent is able to overtrump, then you were scheduled to lose the heart finesse anyway, but you cannot allow your opponent to win with a small trump. (12) One each in hearts and diamonds. (13) Taking finesses. (14) Hearts. (15) You wish to know the location of the heart king before deciding which way to take the finesse in diamonds. (16) The opening bidder must have the diamond queen, since without that card he would not have an opening bid. (17) Your contract is secure no matter who has the diamond queen as you will have at most three losers.

AN OPPONENT HAS OPENED A PREEMPTIVE BID

With a good hand and a long suit: Bid.

With a strong hand and the unbid suits: Double.

The bidding has gone:

Opponent	Partner	Opponent	You
3♥	Pass	Pass	3♠
Pass	4♠	Pass	Pass
Pass			

Here is your hand and your dummy:

Dummy
♠ A763
♥ 72
♦ 8764
♣ KQJ

(18) What are your sure losers? _____

(19) What are your possible losers? _____

_____

You
♠ KJ10982
♥ 53
♦ KJ
♣ A98

Your left hand opponent cashes two high hearts and shifts to a club.

(20) Will your contract depend on a correct guess in the dia-

mond suit? _____

(21) Why? _____

_____

(22) If you lead a low diamond from dummy and your right hand opponent plays low "smoothly" which card should you play from your hand?

_____

(23) Why? _____

_____

(18) Two hearts and one diamond. (19) One spade and one
additional diamond. (20) Yes. (21) You cannot afford to lose two
diamonds and two hearts. (22) King. (23) With his high hearts AND
the ace of diamonds your left hand opponent would probably have
opened one heart.

LESSON SEVEN

Playing the Percentages

Lacking any other clues from the bidding or preceding play, a wise player uses the percentages when he has to locate a missing honor or set up a suit.

ALWAYS REMEMBER:

AN EVEN NUMBER OF CARDS IS LIKELY TO BE DIVIDED UNEVENLY.

AN ODD NUMBER OF CARDS IS LIKELY TO BE DIVIDED . AS EVENLY AS POSSIBLE.

Thus, if you are missing four cards in a suit, they are more likely to be divided three-one than two-two. The exact percentages are:

    3-1 . . . 50%   2-2 . . . 40%   4-0 . . . 10%

THE ONLY EXCEPTION IS WHEN YOU ARE MISSING TWO CARDS: THERE IS A SLIGHTLY BETTER CHANCE THAT THEY ARE DIVIDED 1-1 THAN 2-0. The percentages are:

    1-1 . . . 52%   2-0 . . . 48%

Number of Cards Outstanding								
2	2-0	48%	1-1	52%				
3	2-1	78%	3-0	22%				
4	3-1	50%	2-2	40%	4-0	10%		
5	3-2	68%	4-1	28%	5-0	4%		
6	3-3	35%	4-2	49%	5-1	14%	6-0	2%
7	4-3	62%	5-2	30%	6-1	7%	7-0	1%
8	5-3	47%	4-4	33%	6-2	17%	7-1	3%
9	5-4	59%	6-3	31%	7-2	9%	8-1	1%
10	6-4	46%	5-5	31%	7-3	18%	8-2	4%
11	6-5	57%	7-4	32%	8-3	10%	9-2	1.4%
12	7-5	46%	6-6	30%	8-4	19%	9-3	4%
13	7-6	57%	8-5	32%	9-4	10%	10-3	1.5%

There is an old bridge saying which concerns the proper play if you are missing a queen when you have the ace, king and jack of a suit.

EIGHT EVER, NINE NEVER.

This means: With eight cards, missing the queen, a finesse is in order, with nine cards play to drop the doubleton queen. It is easy to see why you take a finesse when you are missing five cards, but with four cards out the percentages say that they will divide 3-1 more often than 2-2. However, once both opponents have followed to the lead of the suit, there are now only two cards in their hands, and the percentages favor their being 1-1 rather than 2-0.

Always "PLAY THE PERCENTAGES" where there is no clue:

1. From the bidding indicating placement of honors or distribution.
2. From the opening lead indicating placement of honors or distribution.
3. From the play of the hand so far as to the placement of honors or distribution.

How do you handle each of these combinations, assuming that your opponent plays a small card at his first opportunity?

(1) Dummy
    AJ108
    _____

    You
    K654
    _____

(2) Dummy
    K7653
    _____

    You
    A982
    _____

(3) Dummy
    A98765
    _____

    You
    QJ103
    _____

(4) Dummy
    AJ1087
    _____

    You
    K543
    _____

(1) Play the king, then finesse the jack. (2) Play the ace and then the king (or vice versa). (3) Lead the queen; play low if it is not covered (unless your opponent is the kind who ALWAYS covers queens, in which case play the ace in the hope that your right hand opponent has a singleton king. (4) Play the king and then the ace.

This may seem to be a contradiction of the "EIGHT EVER, NINE NEVER" rule but is based on the fact an opponent holding a doubleton queen-jack could play either card; with the queen or jack alone he must play it and this changes the percentages slightly to favor the finesse, if one is possible.

(5)			(6)		
	North			**North**	
	A10652			AK1095	
West		**East**	**West**		**East**
4		Q	4		Q
	South			**South**	
	K873			8732	

(7)			(8)		
	North			**North**	
	A10652			AK1095	
West		**East**	**West**		**East**
Q		4	Q		4
	South			**South**	
	K873			8732	

(5) When the queen falls under South's king, should South finesse West for the jack? _____

(6) When North's ace is played and East plays the queen should South finesse West for the jack? _____

(7) When South plays the king and West plays the queen is a finesse possible for the jack? _____

(8) When North's ace is played and West plays the queen is a finesse possible for the jack? _____

(9) Why is a finesse not possible in (7) or (8)? _____

_____

(5) Yes. (6) Yes. (7) No. (8) No. (9) If West has a doubleton queen-jack, the jack will appear on the next lead of the suit; if East started with the jack plus two spot cards then a loser is inevitable.

NO-NO'S AGAINST NOTRUMP

DO NOT LEAD THE KING FROM KQxx.
DO NOT LEAD THE QUEEN FROM QJxx
unless partner bid the suit.

LEADS IF PARTNER DOUBLES FINAL CONTRACT

Against notrump:
  Partner's suit
  Your suit
  (If both of you have bid a
    suit, lead yours.)
  Dummy's first suit

Against a freely bid slam:
  An unusual lead
    (usually dummy's
    first suit)

LESSON EIGHT

Safety Plays

AS DECLARER, YOUR FIRST RESPONSIBILITY IS TO
MAKE YOUR CONTRACT. NEVER TRY FOR OVER-
TRICKS IF THEY IN ANY WAY MIGHT JEOPARDIZE
THE CONTRACT. WINNING PLAYERS BID WHAT THEY
CAN MAKE AND MAKE WHAT THEY BID. ALWAYS RE-
MEMBER HOW MANY TRICKS YOU NEED.

A safety play is like an insurance policy. Declarer gives up
one (or more) tricks to protect against a split that would defeat the
contract. First decide how many tricks you can afford to lose in
the suit, then decide on the safest way to play the suit.

Dummy
7532

(1) If you can afford to lose only one trick in this
suit, what is the best line of play?

You
AQ864

_____

_____

(2) If you can't afford to lose any tricks in the suit, what is the
best line of play?

_____

_____

(1) Play the ace. If the king does not appear, go to dummy and lead
toward the queen. This play guards against a bad split with a
singleton king on your left. (2) Lead the two from dummy planning
to finesse the queen and hope the suit breaks 2-2.

44

Dummy
A32
You
KJ54

(3) If you need four tricks in this suit, how will you play? _____

(4) Suppose you need only three tricks from this suit. Can you get them if the suit splits 3-3?

_____

(5) Can you get three tricks if you finesse the jack and it loses to

a doubleton queen? _____

(6) Is there a safety play you can take to get three tricks and

protect against a doubleton queen? _____

_____

(3) Win the ace and lead the two to the jack. If the finesse wins and if the suit breaks 3-3, you will win all four tricks (not very likely but if you need it, play for it). (4) If the suit splits 3-3, you will always win three tricks. (5) No. (6) Play the king and ace first. If the queen does not appear, lead the last card from dummy toward the jack. You make three tricks any time the queen is doubleton, the suit splits 3-3, or on a 4-2 split with the queen on your right.

Another variety of SAFETY PLAY involves giving up a trick that might not otherwise be lost in order to safeguard a contract. This often will enable the declarer to run a long suit when entries are short.

In a notrump contract, with one outside entry, how should these combinations be played for the greatest safety?

(7) Dummy
AJ1098752 _____

You
K _____

(8) Dummy
A109653 _____

You
KQ _____

(9) Dummy
AJ10986 _____

You
K2 _____

(10) Dummy
AK10986 _____

You
Q _____

(7) Overtake the king with the ace and concede a trick to the queen if necessary. (8) Play one honor, then overtake the other honor in the dummy; if the jack does not appear, concede a trick. (9) Play the king, then finesse the jack (take the percentage play when both choices are equally safe). (10) Overtake the queen; concede a trick to the jack (if it doesn't fall).

In a notrump contract, with no outside entry to dummy, how should these combinations be played?

(11) Dummy
AQ764   You need four tricks _____

You
K52   _____

(12) Dummy
AQ764   You need four tricks _____

You
K52   _____

(13) Dummy
AK765   You need four tricks _____

You
432   _____

(14) Dummy
AK765   You need four tricks _____

You
432   _____

(11) Play the king, then concede the next trick to your opponents. (12) You must play the king, queen and ace and hope that the suit has split 3-2. (13) Concede one trick to your opponents and hope that the suit split 3-2. (14) Concede two tricks to your opponents; you will make three tricks even if the suit splits 4-1.

LESSON NINE

Defense: Part One

DETERMINE IF THIS HAND NEEDS ACTIVITY ON YOUR PART, OR IF YOU SHOULD PLAY A PASSIVE GAME, LETTING DECLARER FIND HIS OWN TRICKS.

Points to Consider:

1. **The bidding.**
2. **What will be an effective opening lead?**
3. **Can declarer's line of play be determined? If it can is there a line of defense which will be effective against it?**
4. **Count "SURE" defensive tricks; determine how many other tricks are needed. Where will they come from?**
5. **Determine if declarer has a weak suit. At what point is it right to attack the suit? Which partner should make the attack?**
6. **Watch partner's leads and discards so that there is defensive cooperation.**

When it is your turn to bid, you always have the right to ask for a review of the bidding. If you are on opening lead, you may ask for a review of the bidding before you have made your lead. Declarer may ask for a review of the bidding before he plays the first card from the dummy. Partner of the opening leader may ask for a review of the bidding BEFORE he plays a card to the first trick. After your play to the first trick, you may no longer request a review of the bidding. It is important, for effective defense, to listen to the bidding and use the information to plan your defense.

```
                DUMMY
            ♠ AQ65
            ♥ J
            ♦ Q1087
            ♣ AK43
                    YOU
                    ♠ K74
                    ♥ Q10983
Contract: 3NT       ♦ KJ6
Opening Lead: ♣J    ♣ Q7
```

Partner	Dummy	You	Declarer
	1♦	Pass	1♥
Pass	1♠	Pass	2NT
Pass	3NT	Pass	Pass
Pass			

(1) What cards does partner have in the club suit? _____

(2) Approximately how many points does partner have? _____

(3) How do you know this? _____

(4) Will it be possible for your side to set up and use the club suit if declarer plays a low club from dummy?

(5) Why or why not? _____

_____

(6) What suit presents the best chance for tricks for your side?

_____

(7) Assuming declarer plays the three of clubs at the first trick, what is the best defense?

_____

_____

(1) 10, 9, maybe the 8, and some length. (2) Three or less. (3) Declarer and dummy should total 26 and you have 11. (4) No. (5) Declarer made a good play by refusing the first club trick. It is unlikely that the suit can be set up and used because partner probably does not have an entry. (6) Hearts. (7) Overtake the jack of clubs with the queen and shift to the queen of hearts to squash dummy's singleton jack.

49

CAN YOU DETERMINE DECLARER'S LINE OF PLAY?

WHAT WOULD BE AN EFFECTIVE DEFENSE AGAINST IT?

1. Is this the dummy declarer expected from the bidding?
2. What key cards should he find useful?
3. What constructive plays should I make to give declarer problems?
4. Will a holdup play or an early lead through unsupported honors be effective?
5. If leading through declarer, if certain key cards are not in your hand or the dummy, is it possible that partner has them? Should you lead through declarer's strength (just as partner leads through dummy's)?

COUNT YOUR SURE DEFENSIVE TRICKS

WHERE CAN THE OTHER TRICKS COME FROM THAT YOU NEED TO DEFEAT THE CONTRACT?

WHAT SUIT TO LEAD?

Has partner bid? Lead his suit.

Have you bid? Consider leading your own suit.

Has partner made a takeout double? Lead one of the suits he might hold.

Has partner made a business double? This sometimes calls for a specific lead.

Will there be a short suit in dummy? Lead trump.

Example: 1♥ Pass 1NT Pass
          2♦ Pass Pass Pass

Do you have a short suit? Lead it; you may get a ruff.

Is the contract notrump? In almost all cases, if partner has not bid, make the standard lead.

Is your length in trump? Consider leading a long, strong suit.

Have the opponents bid other suits? Avoid leading a suit bid by the opponents unless you have a very good reason.

Have the opponents bid strongly? Make an aggressive lead.

Have the opponents bid hesitantly? Make a passive lead.

```
                    DUMMY
                    ♠ A65
                    ♥ 75
                    ♦ 942
                    ♣ KQ1093
                            YOU
                            ♠ KQ4
                            ♥ 9843
Contract: 3NT               ♦ 763
Opening Lead: ♠10           ♣ A52
```

Declarer	Partner	Dummy	You
1NT	Pass	3NT	Pass
Pass	Pass		

(8) Which cards does partner probably hold in spades? _____

(9) Does declarer hold the spade jack? _____

(10) What suit presents the greatest danger to your side? _____

(11) Assuming that declarer plays a low spade from dummy and
     you win the queen, what card should you now play?

     _____

(12) Why? _____

     _____

(13) How will partner be able to help you in the planning an
     effective defense?

     _____

(8) Nine and eight. (9) Yes. (10) Clubs. (11) King of spades. (12) You
wish to eliminate declarer's entry to dummy, even though this
may mean presenting declarer with an extra spade trick. (13) He
will tell you how many clubs he has by playing high-low with an
even number and "up the line" with an odd number.

51

LESSON TEN

Defense: Part Two

DOES DECLARER HAVE A WEAK SUIT THAT SHOULD BE ATTACKED?
IF SUCH A WEAK SUIT EXISTS, IS IT RIGHT FOR YOU TO LEAD THE SUIT?

OR

SHOULD PARTNER MAKE THE FIRST LEAD OF THE SUIT?

WHEN PARTNER LEADS TO THE FIRST TRICK, IF YOU CAN WIN THE TRICK, YOU MUST DECIDE WHETHER TO RETURN THE SUIT OR MAKE A SHIFT. YOU SHOULD BASE THIS DECISION ON YOUR ESTIMATE OF WHETH-ER DECLARER CAN IMMEDIATELY TAKE THE NUMBER OF TRICKS HE NEEDS TO FULFILL HIS CONTRACT. IF THE ANSWER IS YES, THEN YOU SHOULD DETERMINE WHAT CARDS PARTNER MUST HAVE TO DEFEAT THE CONTRACT, AND YOU SHOULD ASSUME THAT PARTNER HAS THEM AND PLAY ACCORDINGLY.

WHEN PARTNER MAKES AN OPENING LEAD, DECIDE WHICH CARDS IT IS POSSIBLE FOR HIM TO HOLD, AND USE THIS INFORMATION IN PLANNING YOUR DE-FENSE.

```
            DUMMY
            ♠ KQ6
            ♥ A8
            ♦ J10964
            ♣ 965
                        YOU
                        ♠ A32
                        ♥ KQ10954
Contract: 3NT           ♦ 8
Opening Lead: ♠10       ♣ 743
```

Declarer	Partner	Dummy	You
1NT	Pass	3NT	Pass
Pass	Pass		

(1) What is partner's probable spade holding?_____

(2) Approximately how many points does partner have?

_____

(3) Is there any future in the spade suit? _____

(4) Where are your tricks likely to come from? _____

(5) Where are declarer's tricks likely to come from? _____

(6) How can you set up your suit? _____

(7) What are you depending on partner to hold? _____

_____

(8) If partner does not hold these cards, can the contract be set?

_____

(1) Nine, eight and several smaller cards. (2) Five. Declarer has about 16 points, dummy has ten, and you have nine. (3) No. (4) Hearts. (5) Diamonds and/or clubs. (6) By winning the spade ace and leading the king of hearts. (7) A diamond or club entry and three hearts. (8) No.

THE RULE OF ELEVEN

AGAINST A NOTRUMP CONTRACT (AND NORMALLY WHEN LEADING A LOW CARD FROM A LONG SUIT AGAINST A TRUMP CONTRACT) A COMMON LEAD IS "FOURTH BEST."

WHEN A "FOURTH BEST" LEAD IS MADE, THE RULE OF ELEVEN WILL HELP THE LEADER'S PARTNER (AND THE DECLARER) PLACE MISSING CARDS IN THE SUIT. Once you learn this rule you will wonder how you ever managed without it. Subtract the number of the card which partner leads from eleven. This is the "key" number. Count the number of cards higher than the one partner led that you can see in your hand and the dummy. Subtract this from the "key" number. This remainder is the number of higher cards in this suit in the other concealed hand.

THE RULE OF ELEVEN TELLS YOU HOW MANY CARDS HIGHER THAN THE ONE LED THERE ARE IN THE CONCEALED HAND WHICH HAS NOT YET PLAYED.

EXAMPLE OF THE RULE OF ELEVEN

The contract is three notrump

	Dummy	
	J872	
Lead		**You**
6		**K93**

Declarer plays the seven

$$11 \qquad 5$$
$$-6 \qquad -5$$
$$\overline{5} \qquad \overline{0*}$$

*Declarer has no card higher than the six; if you play the nine, your side will take all of the tricks in the suit. If you play the king on the first trick, dummy's jack will eventually win a trick.

You are defending against a notrump contract:

(9) Partner leads the **6**, dummy has **Q 7 5 2**, you have **K 9 3**, how many higher cards does declarer have in his hand? _____

(10) Partner leads the **6**, dummy has **Q 7 5 2**, you have **K 9 8 3,** how many higher cards does declarer have in his hand? _____

(11) Partner leads the **4**, dummy has **9 8 6 5**, you have **J 3 2**, how many higher cards does declarer have in his hand? _____

(12) You are declarer, the six is led, dummy has the **Q 10 8 7** and you have the **A 4 3** in your hand, how many cards higher than the six does your right hand opponent have? _____

(13) Which card should you therefore play from the dummy?

_____

(14) How many tricks will you be able to take in that suit?

_____

(15) You are declarer and the four is led, dummy has the **J 9 8 6** and you have the **A K 7** in your hand, how many cards higher than the four does your right hand opponent have?

_____

(16) Which card should you play from the dummy, and why?

_____

(9) One. (10) None. (11) Two. (12) None. (13) Seven. (14) Three. (15) None. (16) Either the six or the eight, depending on which hand you wish to have on lead for the next trick.

How many higher cards does declarer have in his hand?

	Partner leads	Dummy	Your holding	
(17)	6	**Q 9 5 4**	**A J 3 2**	_____
(18)	4	**9 8 5**	**Q 10 9 2**	_____
(19)	7	**A 10 9 2**	**J 8 4 3**	_____
(20)	3	**A J 9 4**	**K 10 8 5**	_____
(21)	2	**9 8 7 5 4**	**A J 3**	_____

(22) In example (19) what does partner's lead mean? _____

_____

(23) In example (21), how many cards does partner have in the suit?

_____

(24) How do you know this? _____

(17) One. (18) One. (19) Two, the king and queen. (See answer to #22.) (20) Zero. (21) One. (22) Since the Rule of Eleven shows that this can't be the lead of his fourth best, partner has decided (for some reason) to lead "top of nothing." (23) Four. (24) He led the two and he always leads fourth best.

56

POPULAR BRIDGE CONVENTIONS

Conventions are useful in improving bidding accuracy AND (MOST IMPORTANT) AS A DEFENDER, knowledge of these conventions can help you plan an effective defense.
AS A DECLARER, these conventions may help you to ascertain your opponents' high cards and distribution.

BLACKWOOD CONVENTION

4NT asks for aces	5NT asks for kings
Responses:	Responses:
5♣ — 0 or 4*	6♣ — 0
5♦ — 1	6♦ — 1
5♥ — 2	6♥ — 2
5♠ — 3	6♠ — 3
	6NT — 4

*Blackwood bidder should be able to tell which.

REMEMBER

The Blackwood bidder determines the final contract. A bid of 5NT guarantees that partnership has all four aces.

BLACKWOOD RESPONSES WITH A VOID
(Discuss with partner)

Make your normal bid one level higher, EXCEPT when the bid takes you beyond a small slam in the agreed upon trump suit. The void must be a useful one, as determined by the bidding.

BIDDING OVER BLACKWOOD INTERFERENCE

DOPI (prounced dopey)

D = double with
O = zero aces

P = pass with
I = one ace

With two aces, bid next higher suit.
With three aces, skip a suit.

AN ALTERNATE CONVENTION

DEPO

D = double with
E = even number of aces (0, 2, or 4)

P = pass with
O = odd number of aces (1 or 3)

STAYMAN CONVENTION

1NT — 2♣

**(Do you have a 4-card major? I have at
least one 4-card major and at least 8 points)**

Responses by opener:

2♦ — Sorry, partner, no 4-card major.
2♥ — I have four hearts.
2♠ — I have four spades, and I may also have four hearts.

A 3♣ response to a 2NT opening is also Stayman.

JACOBY TRANSFER BIDS
(In response to one notrump opening)

TO ENABLE THE STRONG HAND
TO BE CONCEALED AND RECEIVE THE OPENING LEAD

RESPONDER

2♣ – Stayman
2♦ – demands 2♥
2♥ – demands 2♠

RESPONDER'S REBIDS AFTER RELAY

Pass	–	Weak one suited hand.
2NT	–	Game invitation with five cards in relayed suit.
3♥/3♠	–	Game invitation with 6+ card suit.
3NT	–	Shows five cards in relayed suit. Partner passes or bids game in suit.
4♥/4♠	–	6+ card suit.

(Jacoby can also be used after a two notrump opening.)

GRAND SLAM FORCE

Jump to 5NT asks for 2 of top 3 honors in the agreed suit. (If no suit has been agreed upon it asks for honors in the suit bid last.)

Responses { With 2 of top 3 honors, bid grand slam.
With 0 or 1, bid small slam.

After Blackwood 4NT, a bid of 6 clubs becomes Grand Slam Force (provided clubs is not the trump suit).

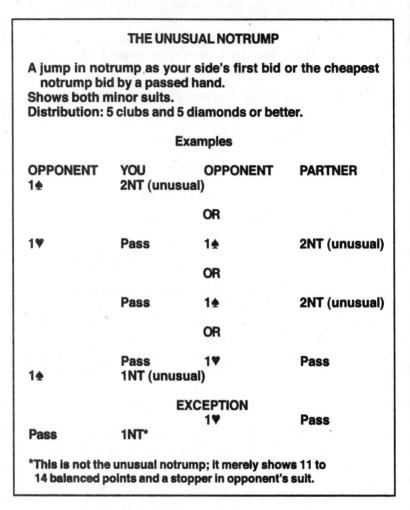

THE UNUSUAL NOTRUMP

A jump in notrump as your side's first bid or the cheapest
  notrump bid by a passed hand.
Shows both minor suits.
Distribution: 5 clubs and 5 diamonds or better.

Examples

OPPONENT	YOU	OPPONENT	PARTNER
1♠	2NT (unusual)		
		OR	
1♥	Pass	1♠	2NT (unusual)
		OR	
	Pass	1♠	2NT (unusual)
		OR	
	Pass	1♥	Pass
1♠	1NT (unusual)		

EXCEPTION

		1♥	Pass
Pass	1NT*		

*This is not the unusual notrump; it merely shows 11 to
  14 balanced points and a stopper in opponent's suit.

HESITATIONS

In a crucial situation, everyone is entitled to have enough time
to consider all the possible alternatives. However, it is incumbent
upon partner not to place undue significance upon your hesita-
tion and to bid only the cards which he can see. If you have
hesitated unduly and are on the borderline of a bid, it is better to
make the bid and take the pressure off partner.

SPLINTER BID BY RESPONDER

A double jump shift showing a singleton or void in suit bid, plus four-card support for partner's major and a minimum of 13 to 15 points. Forcing to game in partner's suit.

OPENER	RESPONDER
1♥	4♦*
OR	
1♠	4♣*
OR	
1♥	3♠*

*Shows four-card support and a singleton or void in bid suit.

SPLINTER BID BY OPENER

A double jump shift guarantees game in partner's suit. Shows a singleton or void in the suit bid.

OPENER	RESPONDER
1♦	1♥
4♣*	

*Shows four hearts and a singleton or void in clubs.

♠ Axx
♥ KQJx
♦ AKJxx
♣ x

AN ADVANCED DEFENSIVE PLAY

The "Queen" Signal

The play of a queen on partner's lead of a king or ace is a special signal which is not utilized too often. It indicates that you are able to win the next round of that suit as you hold either Q J doubleton (or longer), or queen singleton.

EXAMPLE:

North (dummy)
10 8 6

West   East
A K 4 3   Q J

South (declarer)
9 7 5 2

West leads the ace or king, and East plays the queen; West follows with the lead of the three spot.

If West continues with his remaining honor, the A K Q and J will have been played and the defense has set up tricks in the suit for the declarer.

Note: Never use a high-low signal with a holding of Q x!

Playing Honor Cards as A Defender

If your partner or declarer leads a suit and you hold the K Q and must play one of the two cards, always play the lower card to suggest to partner that you may hold the higher card.

This also applies with a K Q J holding; play the jack.

With an A K holding, you win with the king, not the ace.

Playing Honor Cards as A Declarer

When the declarer plays to a trick, he should play his highest honor card if he holds touching honors. Holding A K Q J, he would play the ace; the defenders will not be sure who holds the missing K Q J. Of course, if you can win a trick with an eight or nine, do not play the ace.

Overcalls

It is often difficult to determine when a simple overcall should be made. Vulnerability status is an important factor to consider, as well as partscore.

1. Do *not* use point count valuation for simple overcalls. Consider whether you have a good suit and how many tricks you will be able to take.
2. Do not overcall with a four-card suit or a weak five-card suit.
3. Overcall suits should contain not more than two losers.
4. The rule of two and three is suggested as a guide (to avoid losing more than 500 points). You can afford to go down two tricks doubled, vulnerable or three tricks doubled, not vulnerable.